SLED DOGS

of Denali National Park

by Karen Fortier

Former Kennel Manager, Denali National Park and Preserve

ALASKA GEOGRAPHIC ASSOCIATION

ANCHORAGE, ALASKA

To all the dogs of Denali—past, present, and future

Published by the Alaska Geographic Association in cooperation with Denali National Park and Preserve.

Copyright © 2002 Alaska Geographic Association
Connecting people to Alaska's parks, forests, and refuges.

www.alaskageographic.org

ISBN 978-0-930931-37-7

Library of Congress Control Number: 2001135209

Contemporary photographs: Denali National Park Kennels Collection: pp. ii, 4, 5, 34, 37; Mike Fontaine: p. 9; Jen McWeeny: pp. 1, 13 (left), 35; Stanton Patty: Back cover (author's photograph); Kennan Ward: Cover (dog only); pp. iv, 6, 7, 8, 13 (right, in sidebar), 21, 25, 31, 36, 38; Larissa Yocum: pp. 3, 11, 14, 24, 28, 29, 40, 43

Historical photographs: Denali National Park Archives: pp. 16, 19; University of Alaska (Fairbanks) Rasmussen Library, Alaska and Polar Regions Department: pp. 17 (Charles Bunnel Collection/#69-92-331N), p. 23 (Obey Driscoll Collection/#AC 64-29-192N)

Project Coordinators: Nora Deans, Charlie Loeb, Patricia Harper
Editor: Susan Tasaki
Designer: Jamison Spittler/Jamison Design
Map: Jamison Spittler/Jamison Design, adapted from base created by the Harpers Ferry Center, National Park Service
Illustrations: Donna Gates
Printed in Hong Kong on recycled paper through Global Interprint

CONTENTS

MEET

DENALI'S DOGS

"Ready? Let's go!" A quick tug on the line and the sled is released from the tie-off post. Ten exuberant, barking, leaping sled dogs suddenly become silent and lean into their harnesses. With a burst of energy, the team lunges forward at a run, heading down the trail pulling a fully loaded sled and a well-bundled National Park Service ranger standing on the runners. Soon, a second team takes off behind the lead team. Both are beginning a five-day patrol over mountain passes, along rivers, and across Denali's snow-covered tundra to the Wonder Lake Ranger Station. The sun is shining, the team is happy, and for the rangers, it's hard to imagine wanting to be anywhere or do anything else in the world.

On this patrol the teams will pass through the heart of one of the world's most dramatic expanses of wilderness. The trail they set will snake through the Alaska Range, a land of rugged mountains covered in winter's white blanket, intermittently broken by jagged, dark cliff faces too steep to hold snow. As the teams crest each mountain pass, a new scene of untracked whiteness will

Above: An excited team at hook-up. Once on the trail, the dogs are completely silent.

Left: National Park Service ranger and team on Wonder Lake. Since 1921, sled dogs have been used to patrol Denali National Park.

unfold, and the stunning beauty of the valley below will beckon as they begin their descent.

Rangers and dogs will experience the intense quiet of wilderness, a place so silent that the sound of a twig snapping travels for miles across the treeless landscape. Unless, of course, the wind is howling. Wind is one of several potential hazards that punctuate the beauty and peace of Denali in winter. It blows snow miles from its original resting place, depositing it in valley bottoms and lowland areas; this blowing snow also obscures trails and creates formidable drifts. Teams may encounter an angry moose, one who prefers to stay on the trail rather than flounder in the deep snow; a sudden storm that buries the trail; or a cold snap that sends temperatures plunging to 40 degrees below zero or colder. The challenges and rewards of dog mushing in Denali National Park and Preserve are the stuff of legend.

The sled dogs of Denali have been so important to the park for such a long time that they have become part of the resource, a cultural tradition worthy of protection in its own right. The dogs and the kennels where they live represent important pieces of American history: pre-contact Native American life, the pioneer experience in the far north, and the history of Alaska's first national park. They are the only sled dogs in the United States that help protect a national park and the "scenery and the natural and historic objects and the wildlife therein" — a goal established by the 1916 Organic Act that created the National Park Service — and it has been this way since the park's beginning. When the first rangers started patrolling the then-Mount McKinley National Park in 1921, they used dog teams to reach remote corners of this wilderness to discourage poachers from hunting the park's newly protected wildlife. Over time, the threat from poaching lessened, but as other needs evolved, the dogs remained important and relevant to Denali.

Today, there are winter visitors to contact, trails to break, park wildlife researchers to assist, materials to haul, and boundaries to watch over. All the work must be done in a way that maintains the wilderness ethic of Denali, one of the last places in the world where people can experience a natural landscape almost unaltered by the works of humans, where a natural quiet is uninterrupted by the motors of cars, trains, snowmachines, or even the hum of electric machinery.

The rewards of travelling by dog team can only be achieved if there is mutual respect between the dogs and the musher. Each relies on the other, and over time, a deep level of trust and companionship is reached. It's no wonder that Grant Pearson, one of the earliest rangers (and later superintendent) of the park, chronicled his life here at Denali by writing, "Through it all, the one remembrance that will linger most in my mind is of those years I mushed sled dogs over the wilderness trails of the north country. I'll never forget those huskies and malamutes, my faithful companions of the winter trails, sometimes my only bulwark against utter loneliness."

Now it is your turn to meet the remarkable sled dogs of Denali.

Each of Denali's sled dogs has his or her own unique personality and appearance. Learning individual dogs' strengths and weaknesses is one of the most challenging and rewarding aspects of the musher's job.

What Kind of Dogs are These?

At first glance, sled dogs are an oddly assorted bunch, no two the same. Their coats may be black, white, brown, or gray, or any combination of colors. They may have blue eyes, brown eyes, or occasionally, one of each color. Some have pointy ears, others' ears flop. They certainly don't have the uniform appearance generally seen in movies or depicted in books, and they have no American Kennel Club registration papers.

Most people think of dogs in terms of

breeds. When visitors look at our dogs they often comment that "this one looks like he's part Labrador retriever," or "that one looks like she's got German shepherd in her." Denali's sled dogs are Alaskan huskies, products of a breeding process that is based not upon looks but upon performance.

Sled-dog racing was the force that shaped the dog we call the Alaskan husky. By 1908, when the first organized sled-dog racing event was held, people ran the heartiest of the dogs, many of which were the products of breeding with the native dogs used by the region's indigenous people. By the late 1920s, as racing became more specialized, those who bred sled dogs began introducing other breeds, such as hounds or Irish setters, into the stock. (Contrary to popular belief, huskies are no more closely related to wolves than any other domestic dog. Mushers who experimented with wolf/dog crosses quickly found that the resulting animals were unpredictable and sometimes aggressive. For example, wolf packs are organized in a social system based on a hierarchy of dominance, something that does not work in a sled-dog team.)

Coat color, eye color, and body size and shape vary widely among Alaskan huskies, as they are bred for performance, not appearance.

Dogs from one sled-dog kennel can look very different from those of another, depending on the goals of the individual breeder. Breeders focus on particular physical characteristics that suit their lifestyles and the conditions where they live. For instance, a person in a remote area of Alaska who uses dogs to carry supplies through deep snow would certainly breed a much different-looking dog than someone who competes in sprint races. The former needs a large dog, from 60 to 100 pounds, with a thick coat and long legs. A sprint racer, on the other hand, breeds for speed, gait, and endurance; these dogs tend to be smaller, from 35 to 55 pounds, and more efficient at dissipating heat, as their coats are often somewhat thinner than those of the hauling types.

At the Denali National Park kennels, rangers select for specific attributes in the dogs, and develop the breeding program to achieve those traits. Speed is not one of the priorities of our breeding program. Rather, we need dogs who are even-tempered, personable, and friendly, since they meet thousands of visitors each year. We need dogs who have a good work ethic, who are capable of hauling heavy loads, who work well with other dogs, and who are willing to please. We also need dogs with thick coats that allow them to sleep comfortably out on the trail overnight, and long legs and tough durable feet to break trails through unbroken snow. Since we do not breed for any particular look, Denali's dogs vary widely in appearance.

When deciding which dogs to breed, we choose individuals with these attributes. To help ensure healthy pups, we research both the male and the female's lineage, and sometimes bring in sled dogs from other kennels in order to maintain a diverse gene pool. Each spring a new litter of pups is born at the Denali National Park kennels. Some may become great lead dogs, while others will fill niches as members of the team. Regardless of position, all are crucial to the mission: patrolling Denali's wilderness.

Denali's dogs are characteristically long-legged, an attribute that helps them break trails through deep snow.

THE LIFE OF A

DENALI SLED DOG

Many visitors to Denali's kennels have pet dogs at home, dogs who lounge on the couch, run in the yard, fetch sticks, sleep inside at night, play with the kids—very much members of the family. Most family pets have never seen a harness, much less know what it's like to pull a loaded sled at 20 degrees below zero. Denali's dogs lead considerably different lives than the average family pet. But though they are working dogs, they have distinct personalities and special relationships with the rangers with whom they spend their time.

From the time they're puppies, Denali's dogs are trained and conditioned to pull sleds as part of a team. They're also socialized to be good hosts to kennel visitors, which number in the thousands during the summer months. Summer visitors attend sled-dog demonstrations at the park kennels to learn about the history of Denali's sled dogs and to watch five excited huskies pull a ranger on a wheeled sled around a gravel track. No one quite knows why huskies love to run, but one look at a team being harnessed shows that they love what they do.

Above: *Since 1939, summer visitors have enjoyed sled dog demonstrations at the historic park kennels; these demonstrations are Denali's most popular interpretive program.*

Left: *When not out on patrol, Denali's dogs enjoy relaxing in the sunshine on top of their dog houses.*

The lives of Denali's sled dogs begin at the kennels themselves, where most of the puppies are born. The pups spend their first two months of life nursing and sleeping, gaining several pounds per week. At four weeks, they begin to eat commercial dog food, and they are fully weaned at six weeks.

Throughout this time, the puppies are handled by adults and children, socialized to be comfortable with all the people they will come into contact with during the summer months. The pups' feet and mouths are regularly examined to accustom them to having booties put on and their teeth examined when they're older.

Soon, they venture out of their pen, exploring the outside world. Kennel staff take the puppies for walks, giving them opportunities to

Each spring, a new litter of puppies is born. The pups' names are chosen following a unique theme, such as trees, wildflowers, or mountain ranges.

explore puddles, climb steep slopes, and amble over willow bushes and tundra. This familiarizes the puppies with the environment and helps them become confident and secure in their surroundings. During this time they are also allowed to begin interacting with the adults in the dog yard. Tentative at first, they are soon playing and romping. Throughout these early months, the pups are taught common commands such as sit, come, and stay; correct responses earn them biscuits or verbal praise. Their individual personalities develop: some of the pups are bold and confident, others are rambunctious, and others want nothing more than to please you. By six months of age, they are two-thirds of their full adult weight.

Running isn't the only thing—Denali kennel staff make sure their sled dogs are well socialized to people during the pups' critical early months.

A PUPPY BECOMES A SLED DOG

When the snow begins to fall, the level of excitement among the dogs builds and fall training begins. The pups, by now six months old, watch as the adult dogs are harnessed for early-season training runs. Then it's their turn. At first they run loose beside or behind the team, observing the adult dogs and experiencing a variety of winter conditions—glare ice, blowing snow, wind crust, overflow. After a few weeks, they too are harnessed, though not attached to the sled. The pups are amusing to watch as they bound along with the team, chasing and tackling each other, happy, rolling balls of snow and fur. Already, the confident pups—who sometimes run out in front of the lead dogs—stand out. Within a month of running loose with the team, some of the pups fit themselves into an empty spot and run in formation with the other dogs,

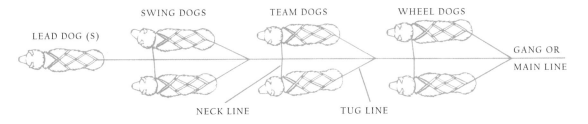

Sled dogs are assigned team positions according to an assessment of their particular strengths; each position contributes to the success of the team as a whole.

demonstrating that they are ready to be part of the team.

When the pups are six months old, they are harnessed with the team for short runs. Positioned next to well-trained adult dogs, they learn much of what it takes to become a sled dog from their furry mentors. Occasionally, they chew on lines or harnesses, play with the dogs running next to them, and are distracted by new sights such as other dog teams—too much goofing off earns the pups a gentle nip from exasperated adults.

With the expert guidance the older dogs provide, the pups develop into working sled dogs very quickly. By the end of their first winter, they will already have several hundred miles of experience running in harness. As their ancestors have done since Denali's beginning, they will have run on glare ice of frozen rivers, wind-sculpted snow of the tundra, and deep unconsolidated snow in the spruce forests.

By the pups' second winter, they may be ready for the challenge of seeing what it's like to be a lead dog. Commonly, a younger, inexperienced dog is placed next to a mature leader. Lead dogs are confident, focused, willing to run out in front of the other dogs, and able to understand and follow the musher's verbal commands. Swing (the position directly behind the lead dogs) is a good position for leaders-in-training; from this vantage point, they can hear the commands and see how the dogs directly in front of them respond. Some dogs are great trail leaders, while others excel at setting a trail in unmarked snow. Each dog has his or her own individual strengths. Working with each to identify these strengths is one of the most rewarding aspects of the musher's job. The training of Denali's dogs is a process that continues throughout their lives.

SEASONS OF A SLED DOG

As adults, Denali sled dogs settle into a routine that is fairly predictable from year to year. During the summer, when it's too hot for serious exercise, they spend their days running the demonstration loop for kennel visitors. In the long summer evenings, volunteers take the dogs for "walks," during which the powerful huskies drag their companions down the edge of the park road. This popular volunteer program not only provides the dogs with exercise and a chance to get away from the kennels, but also forges special bonds between the dogs and their walkers, bonds that sometimes last for years.

During summer sled-dog demonstrations, visitors get the thrill of watching five excited huskies pull a ranger around a gravel track on a wheeled sled.

Once the summer season ends, it is time for fall training to begin. Denali rarely has enough snow to run dogs with a sled until early November, but training must begin much sooner. Using a park campground for these conditioning excercises, the mushers hook six to ten dogs to an all-terrain vehicle or a four-wheeler and take them on gradually lengthening work-out runs. Though not nearly as peaceful as sled runners gliding smoothly over snow, these training runs are crucial in providing the exercise necessary to rebuild the dogs' muscle and endurance, which diminish during the summer months. It's also good preparation for the heavy sleds they will pull later in the winter.

As soon as there's enough snow, the sleds are brought out and the real winter excitement begins! During November and December, temperatures drop to the minus-20s, -30s, and sometimes -40s, and daylight lasts only four hours. Patrol trips can range from one day to many weeks. As the dogs' endurance increases and the rivers freeze, patrols push farther into the heart of Denali wilderness. Late February and the month of March are the height of the winter season for trips into the park, both for visitors and park personnel working on research and other projects. At this time of year, dog teams spend solid weeks on patrol. At least one team, and often more, is based at the Wonder Lake Ranger Station deep inside the park.

By early April, the temperature rises, the river ice diminishes, and the snow turns slushy. Now the teams return home to the kennels at park headquarters. It is time to give the dogs a break, put away the harnesses and other winter gear, and prepare for another summer season in Denali National Park.

THE RETIREMENT YEARS

The average working life of a Denali dog is typically from eight to nine years. Once a dog reaches this age, rangers keep an eye on its levels of enthusiasm and stamina.

When a dog starts slowing down or losing interest in work, an adoptive home is found in the local community or another northern locale. Often, volunteer dog-walkers who have developed special relationships with their dogs will want to adopt them. Since

Once retired from the kennels, sled dogs like ten-year-old Mystic are adopted; for the rest of their days, they spend their time relaxing, hiking, or playing with their new families.

they are so well socialized throughout their lives at the kennels, Denali dogs usually make outstanding companions once they are ready to retire. After their years of hard work, they settle into lives of relative luxury, sometimes purely as pets, sometimes as part of a less-demanding recreational team. The legacy of the sled dogs of Denali is then carried on by the younger generations.

Overflow

Overflow, a condition frequently encountered in Denali during the winter, often provides exciting challenges for winter travelers. When a thick layer of ice forms on the surface of rivers or lakes, it constricts the space available for the water below. As pressure builds, the water needs some place to go. Eventually it will break through even a thick ice layer and spill onto the surface. Depending on the

air temperature, the water will either freeze (sometimes forming peculiar-looking glaciers that build up layer upon layer over time) or will flow over the surface of the ice.

What Does It Take to Be a Lead Dog?

One of greatest rewards for any dog musher is to see the efforts of his or her training and breeding produce a great lead dog. Very strong bonds develop between mushers and their lead dogs. The musher is like a manager or coach, selecting individuals who will perform well and helping them toward success. To raise a pup who later becomes a confident, focused, intelligent adult dog willing to run out in front of the team takes an enormous amount of training. Though every musher would like to raise a whole litter of pups who become leaders, not all pups have the personality required for this role—those dogs will take up other important positions on the team. (On the rare occasion that a dog shows little aptitude for being a sled dog, he or she is placed in a home as a pet.)

Lead dogs are confident and focused, and understand the musher's voice commands. Each lead dog has different strengths and it is the musher's job to identify them and help the dog be successful.

Lead dogs are chosen and then trained for the position based on observed talent. Contrary to popular belief, lead dogs are not chosen because they establish dominance over the rest of the team; in fact, dominance of any type among the dogs is discouraged. Nor are they the biggest or toughest individuals. Trained to understand the directional voice commands given by the musher, lead dogs are the team's steering wheels. They are taught to hold the gang line tight when the team is being hooked up as well as when they're stopped on the trail. A loose gang line results in big spaghetti-like tangles of dogs and lines, something every musher tries to avoid. Lead dogs are trained to stop the team when the musher says "Whoa," and to wait until the musher says "Ready?" or "Let's go!" Focused either on the trail ahead of them or the commands of the musher if they are running through untracked snow, lead dogs guide the team confidently across river ice and are not intimidated by overflow or open stream channels. They are not easily distracted by wildlife, loose pups, or other teams out on the trail.

While training young dogs, it is important to set them up for success. During a young dog's first few times in lead, the musher makes sure things will not be too challenging or stressful. Gradually, mushers expose the novice sled dogs to increasingly challenging trail conditions.

Mushers have different philosophies about when it is appropriate to put a young dog in lead for the first time. Generally, by the second winter, a young dog will be placed alongside an experienced adult lead dog. By this time, the dog has already been in other positions in the team and so has experience as a sled dog. The first few times in lead are usually exciting for the potential leaders. Some take right to the challenge of running in front of the team. Others may be a bit unsure of themselves, looking back at the musher as though to say, "Are you sure you want me up here?" They may not know the commands, but as their co-leaders respond, these dogs pick up the skills of their mentors.

DOG HISTORY

Sled dogs are one of the threads that connect the larger history of Denali and Alaska. Judge James Wickersham said it well in 1938: "He who gives time to the study of the history of Alaska, learns that the dog, next to man, has been the most important factor in its past and present development." That statement holds true at Denali National Park. The dogs' trusty paws have guided rangers patrolling Denali's wilderness since the park was founded.

Even before this expansive land of glaciers, tundra, rivers, and mountains was designated a national park, sled dogs were very much part of the landscape. Prior to the 1800s, Athabaskan Indian tribes—nomadic groups who used dogs primarily as pack animals—searched for fish and game in the Denali region. By the early 1900s, sled dogs provided the primary transportation and freighting method for miners seeking gold in the Kantishna Hills. When naturalist Charles Sheldon needed a guide to assist with his studies of Dall sheep in Denali country during the winter of 1907–1908, he hired veteran Alaskan dog musher Harry Karstens, whose dog teams freighted supplies and provided transportation for research and hunting. Sheldon was so

Above: Mr. and Mrs. Carl Sesui and their dogs, March 1919. Athabascans living in the Denali region used dogs to extend their hunting ranges and to haul supplies long before Denali National Park was created.

Left: Fritz Nyberg and Bos'n, his lead dog, 1927. Nyberg, one of Denali's earliest rangers, and Bos'n traveled thousands of miles together during the 1920s.

enchanted with the mountains and wildlife that when he returned to the East Coast, he lobbied Congress to set this area aside as a national park, a long campaign that finally came to successful resolution with the establishment of Mount McKinley National Park in 1917.

Karstens and his sled dogs participated in the first successful attempt to climb Mount McKinley in 1913. On that expedition, sled dogs hauled supplies from the town of Nenana to the head of the Muldrow Glacier, 11,500 feet up the slopes of McKinley. Although Sheldon never returned to the park he helped establish, Karstens and his sled dogs remained significant participants in the park's early development. It was 1921 before the first ranger was hired, and that ranger was none other than Harry Karstens. Among his duties was to bring poaching of the park's wildlife under control. Caribou, moose, and Dall sheep were being hunted throughout the northern drainages of the park to feed settlers in Fairbanks and other gold camps, as well as the thirty or more dog teams in the Mount McKinley area. The levels of poaching were devastating to the park's wildlife. Karstens, who knew that the best way to travel in this frozen country was on a sled behind a team of enthusiastic huskies, founded the park kennels to ensure a reliable supply of healthy, well-trained, working dogs.

Sled dogs made it possible for the rangers to patrol the park's boundaries, record wildlife populations, and keep in touch with the nearby residents. As his son, Eugene, who was a child in Denali during the early 1920s, reflected in a memoir, "When I was old enough Father took me along when he went on patrol, with the team of dogs we would be gone for several days at a time. I would be in the sled all bundled up in blankets and furs and packed in with the provisions."

Over the next few years, more rangers were hired and the park kennels were expanded. Each ranger was assigned a team of seven dogs and a district of the park that they were responsible

Fritz Nyberg, shown here ca. 1923 at the Boundary Creek Cabin, occupied much of his time with patrols, poachers, and cabin-building. Sled dogs were integral to all these activities.

for patrolling in the winter. Ranger Grant Pearson, who was hired by Karstens in 1926, recalls being told that he was lacking in experience but considered capable of learning. To test him out, Karstens said, "I'll send you on a patrol trip alone. You will be gone a week. If you don't get back by then I'll come looking for you, and you had better have plans made for a new job."

Patrols lasted months at a time; in between, rangers would return to Headquarters, restock provisions, and head out once again. With the assistance of the dogs, who pulled the supply-loaded sleds and hauled logs, these pioneer rangers also constructed cabins along the boundaries to provide shelter for them and their dogs while they were out on patrol. During construction of the park road between 1923 and 1938, the Alaska Road Commission also built 14-by-16-foot log cabins through the interior of the park, which served as cookhouses in the summer and storage houses in the winter. As camps were abandoned after the road's completion, these cabins were converted to patrol shelters.

By the late 1920s, the kennels were thriving, and in 1929, the present kennel building was constructed. By 1936, fifty dogs and fourteen pups were housed and cared for at the National Park Service kennels, and they soon became one of the most popular summertime attractions for the increasing numbers of tourists who were finding their way to the park. In 1939, Superintendent Frank Been noted this phenomenon in a memorandum to the Director of the

National Park Service: "A feature of constant attraction to which many visitors return during their stay in the park is the kennels of Alaskan huskies. These fine friendly animals are always glad to see the visitors, as the latter are the former." He went on to say, "As dog teams are giving way to airplanes, we hope that the McKinley Park huskies will always be retained as part of the historical interest of the park as well as of the Territory."

The next decade brought great changes throughout the world and at Mount McKinley National Park. The United States entered World War II, and airplanes began replacing dogs as the mode of mail transportation throughout Alaska. Labor and budget shortages during the war years made it difficult to maintain an active sled-dog kennel facility, and by 1949, the last of Mount McKinley's sled dogs were gone. Snow jeeps were used briefly in the 1950s, but mechanized equipment proved unreliable in the extreme temperatures and weather conditions of the Alaskan interior.

In 1950, the park acquired a surplus army dog team that was used for visitor programs and the occasional winter patrol; commitment to the kennels fluctuated, depending upon the interest of park personnel and park management. However, over the course of the next three decades, several new federal laws led to a renaissance of interest in the sled dogs and strengthened National Park Service commitment to their presence in the park. The National Historic Preservation Act (1966) was the first. This act declared that "the historical and cultural foundations of the Nation should be preserved as a living part of our community life and development in order to give a sense of orientation to the American people."

This mandate—combined with the dogs' proven reliability and adaptability to all types of terrain, weather, and conditions—provided the official rationale for their continued use. By the early 1970s, the dogs were once again a vital part of the park's winter operations. The first full-time kennel manager was hired in 1974 to oversee the care, breeding, training, and exercising of the dogs; to instruct rangers in the skill of dog driving; and to oversee in the operation of the summer sled-dog demonstrations.

In 1980, a second incentive for using sled dogs at the park was provided with the passage of the Alaska National Interest Lands Conservation Act (ANILCA). This legislation tripled the size of Mount McKinley National Park, changed its name to Denali National Park and Preserve, and designated the original 2-million-acre park as wilderness. According to the 1964 Wilderness Act, wilderness is "an area where the earth and its community of life are untrammeled by man, where man himself is a visitor who does not remain." In short, it is an area to be protected and managed so as to preserve its natural conditions. This new legal designation restricted such activities as the use of motorized equipment and mechanized transport. For rangers, travel by dog sled allowed them to continue carrying out the park's mission during the winter months by means that were consistent with the spirit of ANILCA and the Wilderness Act.

Of Denali's 6 million acres, 2 million are designated as wilderness. Henry David Thoreau said that "in wildness is the preservation of the world"; the National Park Service made a commitment to that preservation by setting aside and protecting this vast Alaskan landscape.

Today, Denali's dogs continue to do their jobs of providing transportation for rangers during the winter. On average, 3,000 patrol miles are logged throughout the park's interior, all on the back of sleds pulled by NPS huskies. During the summer, attendance at the daily sled demonstrations totals over 50,000 annually. However, it is in the wintertime that Denali's sled dogs prove, with each day of eager service, that they are the heart of a tradition and the true symbol of the Denali wilderness.

History of Sled Dogs

It is unclear when and where the idea of dogs pulling sleds originated. Anthropologists speculate that northern-dwelling Paleolithic hunter-gatherers first domesticated various subspecies of wolves 10,000 to 15,000 years ago. Over the next several thousand years, the role of domestic dogs evolved, and archeological evidence indicates that by A.D. 1000, people living along the Alaska coast probably used dogs to pull sleds. It is likely that the idea found its way across the Bering Sea into Alaska from northern Eurasia. These animals, who were not pets, were kept by northern people to assist in obtaining food and other essential materials needed for survival. The dogs allowed hunters to travel greater distances in search of wild game; by extending their hunting ranges, these early people were able to improve their survival rate in the unforgiving far north.

When explorers, hunters, and trappers of European descent began moving into Alaska, they learned from the native people that the best way to travel around in a frozen, snow-covered land was by dog sled. Dogs were so useful to newcomers that by the end of the nineteenth century, dog teams were the primary means of carrying people, mail, and supplies between the settlements and gold-mining towns that were springing up throughout Alaska.

The gold rush across Canada's Yukon Territory and Alaska between 1880 and 1908 drastically changed both the country and the dogs. Hopeful gold-seekers brought Saint Bernards, Newfoundlands, retrievers, spaniels, hounds, and any other dog that might pull a sled into the north country. Demand for sled dogs was so high that it was said that no dog was safe on the streets of seaport towns from San Francisco to Seattle. A miner destined for the Yukon might pay $250 for a dog that could be relied upon to pull. During and after the gold rush, geographers, biologists, mail carriers, and trappers all depended on their trusty teams of dogs to get them safely from place to place in the course of their work.

In 1925, the world's attention focused on the single most famous sled-dog feat in history. People in the town of Nome on Alaska's northwest coast were stricken with diphtheria, and desperately needed an antitoxin. No roads went to Nome, available open-cockpit planes were thought incapable of making the trip because of the temperatures, and boats were prevented from reaching the town by the winter's pack ice. So on January 27, the antitoxin was handed off a railroad car to a dog musher in Nenana, just 60 miles north of the Mount McKinley National Park entrance, and the "Race for Life" began. Twenty individual sled-dog teams relayed the antitoxin 674 miles to Nome in just six days through some of the worst of Alaska's winter weather. They reached Nome in time to save many lives, thus placing a heroic exclamation mark at the end of an era of transportation by dog sled.

This turn-of-the-century mail driver is likely to have netted an annual salary of $2,225; sled-dog teams delivered the mail throughout Alaska as recently as 1963.

Indeed, as Alaska became more settled over the course of the twentieth century, airplanes, snowmachines, railroads, and roads dramatically diminished the need for sled dogs. Dog teams might have gone the way of the horse-drawn stagecoach were it not for sled-dog racing. The first organized sled-dog race, the All-Alaska Sweepstakes, was held in Nome in 1908. Since then, sled-dog racing has evolved into a highly competitive sport of long-distance (1,000 miles), mid-distance (300 to 500 miles), and sprint (25 miles) events. Today, sled-dog racing is the official sport of the state of Alaska and is the primary force shaping the world of sled-dog nutrition, breeding, and training. It has inspired many recreational mushers, people who use dog teams for winter outdoor adventure, fun, and companionship. Only beyond the edge of the roads, in towns and villages largely inhabited by Native Alaskans, are there still a few people who use dog teams as their primary mode of transportation for hunting and trapping, carrying on the traditions of Alaska's very first dog mushers.

SLED

DOG PATROLS

Across the sparkling snow-covered tundra the sled runners glide. The eight dogs pulling the sled have traveled twenty miles since morning. Every few miles, the musher calls "Whoa," a signal for them to stop and rest. The dogs bite a few mouthfuls of snow, eat a high-calorie fat snack, roll onto their backs and wiggle around, and then leap back to their feet. Lunging in their harnesses, they're anxious to be moving down the trail once again.

It is December, and the angle of the sun does not rise high enough to reach above the mountains. The brief daylight hours pass in continual sunset, and pastel light streaks the sky and mountains. A few miles ahead is a patrol cabin stocked with winter provisions; a mere flick of a match provides warmth, dry clothes, food, and water.

Not only has the purpose of Denali's sled-dog patrols remained relatively unchanged since the park's founding in 1917, but the entire experience of traveling by dog team through Denali National Park has remained the same. Rangers patrolling in Denali are still at the whim of the often bitter cold, the short days, and the wind that can pick up in an

Above: *Though the majority of patrols go from cabin to cabin, rangers and teams sometimes camp out in order to access more remote areas of the park.*

Left: *On a crystal-clear day, the team crests a rise in full view of Denali. Storms and blowing snow can change a scene like this in a matter of minutes.*

instant and sweep across the mostly treeless landscape. Rangers are still faced with age-old dangers: encountering an angry moose on the trail, getting caught in a storm, or plunging through the river ice.

So why, in this modern age, do we continue to use such an archaic means of transportation?

One of the purposes of a national park is to preserve historic and natural resources for the benefit of future generations. The use of sled dogs to access the wilderness not only preserves an important cultural resource, but also provides a reliable means of transportation and allows rangers at Denali to be the eyes and ears of the park during the long winter months. Similar to summer's backcountry rangers, rangers using dog teams are able to contact winter recreationists and provide information on trail conditions, offer assistance, and monitor use in a low-impact style that preserves the wilderness spirit essential to Denali. The presence of the rangers in the backcountry helps deter illegal activities in the park, such as poaching or riding snowmachines. The sled-dog trails made during winter patrols are used by winter recreationists who want to explore Denali on skis, snowshoes, or with their own dog team. Denali's dogs also provide transportation for some of the park researchers who collect data on wildlife populations during the winter months. Over the years, the dogs have hauled thousands of pounds of materials, supplies for cabin building or restoration projects or trail construction efforts. They are very much a key part of park operations.

Apart from functional reasons, there are many other practical reasons why Denali continues to use dogs. The dogs have the uncanny ability to find a patrol cabin during a whiteout, sensing the snow- or wind-obscured trail beneath their paws. They run through overflow without getting bogged down, they don't run out of gas or have mechanical parts that freeze up, and they help preserve the natural quiet in a world where silence is an increasingly scarce resource.

PATROL LIFE

Denali's sled-dog patrols last anywhere from a single day to up to six weeks. The trail through the park's wilderness core roughly follows the park road corridor from park headquarters to Wonder Lake and Kantishna. The historic patrol cabins that serve as quarters for seasonal rangers in the summer provide shelter for the rangers out on winter patrol.

Some days, everything goes just right: deep-blue sky, no wind, and a beautiful trail stretching out in front of the dogs, happy huskies trotting along in synchrony, a proud young female demonstrating that she has what it takes to be a leader. The occasional chirp of a boreal chickadee and the swish of the sled runners gliding over the surface of the snow are the only sounds. Not all days on the trail are smooth sailing, though. Some days, everything seems too hard, too tough, too much work! These are the days when the sled flips on a bulge in the river ice and the musher is dragged along for several hundred yards before managing to right the sled and stand back on the runners. It seems like too much work on the days when there are three feet of powdery snow and it's too deep for the dogs, so the musher has to snowshoe ahead of the team for miles and miles to the next patrol cabin. Some days the lead dogs don't follow the commands and it's a struggle to make the least amount of progress. The good days are definitely not the ones when the sled smacks into a big spruce tree and a runner breaks fifty miles out from headquarters. But somehow, through all these hardships, there is nothing quite like the reward of making it all work when it's just the musher, the dogs, the land, and the elements.

Weather conditions, which vary greatly from year to year in Denali, are the main factor that determines the types of

obstacles the mushers will encounter out in the park. In years with little snow, hazards in the trail—boulders, tree roots, and overflow ice—seem to wait for a chance to break a sled. Descending an almost snow-free mountainside or some of the park's notoriously ice-filled canyons can cause a sled to go careening out of control. Making it safely to the bottom with musher, dogs, and sled intact seems somehow miraculous. The deep-snow years make controlling the sled much easier but make travel more exhausting for both the dogs and the mushers. Breaking a trail on snowshoes in front of a dog team makes for a very long day indeed!

Like snow conditions, Denali's temperatures are quite variable. A typical day might be minus 20 degrees F during the middle of winter, with extremes between minus 50 to plus 40 degrees F. Sled travel is generally restricted to between minus 30 and plus 30 degrees F, more for the safety and comfort of the mushers than for the dogs. Mushers and dogs risk frostbite when running at temperatures below minus 40 degrees. On the other extreme, the dogs risk overheating if running in temperatures much above 30 degrees.

AT THE PATROL CABIN

After a long day on the trail, both rangers and dogs are happy to arrive at the patrol cabin. First, the dogs are transferred to a cable line attached between two trees, with individual drop lines for each dog; here, they'll sleep soundly throughout the night, protected by their thick,

Above: *The best view from any dog yard in the world: evening alpenglow casts beautiful shades on Denali from the Wonder Lake Ranger Station during a March patrol.*

Left: *Patrol cabins offer needed respite along the trail. Spaced about a day's "mush" apart, the cabins provide provisions such as dog food, which are stocked prior to winter so that patrols can last longer and go farther.*

What do we carry in the sled?

Although provisions for both the dogs and the mushers are stocked in the patrol cabins during the fall, it is necessary to carry many survival items in the sled as well, as mushers must always be prepared to camp out on the trail. Typically, each sled carries the following items:

* extra clothes
* sleeping bag
* small camping stove
* axe
* snowshoes
* maps
* compass
* fire starter
* headlamps and extra batteries
* a bucket for melting snow
* first aid supplies for dogs and the musher
* food for dogs and the musher
* dog food bowls
* booties for the dogs
* tools and repair supplies for the sleds
* extra ropes and harnesses

two-layered coats. A testimony to the insulating capacity of the husky coat, new-fallen snow piles up on the dogs without melting, giving them a pocket of extra insulation while they sleep.

After the dogs are secured, there begins the seemingly endless process of melting gallons and gallons of snow. A fire is started in the cabin's stove and snow collected in five-gallon metal buckets is put on to melt. It can take ten to fifteen gallons of snow to make one gallon of water. Each dog requires approximately four quarts of water per day to stay well hydrated in the dry winter air. While this is in process, sleds are unpacked, harnesses are brought in to dry, the dogs' feet are checked for abrasions, and sleds and lines are inspected to make sure that no bolts have rattled loose and they are safe to use the next day.

Once the water's warm, feeding begins. Sled dogs, like human athletes, must eat a high-quality, balanced diet. At Denali, the dogs' diet consists primarily of a commercial dog food formulated for working dogs, made largely of poultry meal, fish meal, rice, and fat. The dogs process fat in much the same way as humans process carbohydrates, and it is important that they receive adequate amounts. Since water tends to freeze in the bowls, the dry food is soaked in warm water, which creates a rich, brothy stew that the dogs gobble down in seconds. During the winter, the dogs consume 3,000 to 4,000 calories per day, as much as 5,000 if it is very cold or they are working particularly hard.

It is a rule of the north that the dogs eat first. Once the dogs have been fed, the mushers can feed and hydrate themselves. Since most of the food is stocked in the cabins in the fall, it seems like Christmas when the rangers tear into the food boxes to find out what they'll be eating. The food ranges from cans of beef stew to pasta to boxes of macaroni and cheese. It's generally limited to dried, canned, or non-perishable foods. Occasionally, a truly tasty meal will be brought along on the sled—frozen vegetables or a thick T-bone steak. There is one item that is almost never missing from cabin larders: powdered drink mixes or teas to mask the sometimes odd-tasting water made from the melted snow (which is sometimes "seasoned" with bits of spruce nee-dles and the occasional snowshoe hare pellet). Evenings are when har-nesses are repaired and dogs are brought inside to lounge around and get lots of affection.

During winter, the dogs eat a high-calorie food soaked in warm water to help keep them well hydrated. Each dog drinks approximately four quarts of water each day.

Crawling out of their sleeping bags into the chill of the patrol cabin the next morning, the rangers begin preparing the dogs' morning meal. Again, the dry food is soaked in warm water and portioned out among the dogs. After the morning chores are completed and the sleds are loaded and secured to a tree, the dogs once again begin their excited sled-dog song and dance, and a new day on the trail begins.

Tales of Denali's Pioneer Rangers

Mount McKinley National Park's first superintendent, Harry Karstens, had a difficult task. Not only did he have to protect the park's wildlife, but he also had to find the right people to get the job done. Rangers at the park needed to be tough and willing to live in the extreme cold for weeks at a time. They needed to be sturdy and self-reliant enough to travel alone, build log cabins, manage a dog team, and deal with poachers. Among the men who survived this weeding-out process were Fritz Nyberg, Grant Pearson, Al Winn, E. R. McFarland, Bob Degan, and Lou Corbley.

The primary goal of all the patrols was to ensure that moose, caribou, and sheep were safe from poachers. Sometimes, the rangers only found the evidence of a kill, other times they were able to arrest an illegal hunter. Most often, they informed hunters where the park boundaries lay. Their mere presence was itself a deterrent to poaching.

Chronicled in superintendent's reports throughout the 1920s and 1930s are stories of these pioneer rangers, tales that depict the tough conditions, hard work, and devotion and determination of both the rangers and their dogs.

November 11, 1924

Rangers Nyberg and Degan returned at 6 p.m., having come from Cantwell today, a distance by trail of over 30 miles. That is very good travelling considering the softness of the dogs (early season), who arrived home feeling playful and in good shape. The boys report quite a number of idle men around Windy and Cantwell but no evidence of any hunting going on in or near the park. They report seeing large numbers of caribou and sheep, but they were all in or near the park line. Nyberg and Degan bought a good lead dog, to fill in their team, which they will turn over to the park.

November 17, 1924

Left Healy at 5 a.m. with dogteams and went to forks of Dry creek where we thought the hunter might be located. I backtracked at the crossing of Dry creek and picked up a man's trail on the gravel bar which was bare of snow. With much trouble I followed this trail until I came in sight of a small cabin. On the other side of the cabin I saw a man some distance away who had just left the cabin and was going up in the hills. I followed him some distance until I saw him start to haul out a sheep carcass. Then I came up to him and took him in charge. There was a second sheep on the roof of the cabin and the cabin was 2 miles in the park. I loaded his outfit on my sleigh and took him to Healy, arriving there after dark.

November 30, 1924

Ranger Nyberg left Savage camp at 8 a.m. Went down through Savage canyon to northern boundary. Not safe to go through canyon with dogs hooked to sleigh as there is much open water and big boulders. Had to push sleigh through letting the dogs follow. No evidence of anyone hunting. Saw 30 sheep in canyon.

January 1931

On January 24, Acting Chief ranger Corbley and myself departed from headquarters for a trip along the east and south boundary of the park, Windy station being our objective point. It took us three and one-half days on account of the deep snow, and owing to the fact that the snow had never crusted due to the mild winter. Ordinarily this trip is made in a day and one-half, but we had to break trail for two days with snow shoes going ahead of the dog teams. On the third night we were caught high up in the mountains in Windy Pass, and as the dogs were played out it was necessary for us to make a camp high above the timber line. This is a pleasure that only an Alaskan can appreciate.

After several years of vigilance, the rangers drastically reduced the level of poaching within Mount McKinley National Park boundaries. When we applaud the work of Denali's sled dogs through the park's history, it is important to also recall their mushers, who deserve an equal share of praise for their service.

LIV

Stepping inside the historic kennel building at park headquarters, visitors are often struck with a profound sense of history. The feeling comes not just from the log walls; or the historic leather harnesses hung up on pegs; or the odors of dog food, dog fur, and harness oil in the air. Though all of these things contribute to the kennels' aura, the most powerful cues come from the wooden nameplates that hang on the beams above the workbenches, tools, and harnesses, nameplates of the dogs who once lived and worked at Denali National Park: Taiga and Tundra, Fudge and Lic'rice, Cassi and Gale, Chaos and Havoc, Mitts and Suzie, to name a few. Look up at the names and imagine Tige determinedly leading his team to safety after they fell through river ice into deep water, saving his musher's life. Or Gem'ni lying happily under the blankets in a patrol cabin bed after a long day on the trail. Or Suzie curled up with a litter of pups who would become the great-grandparents and grandparents of the dogs who live in the kennels today.

All of these individuals, these sled dogs working together with their National Park Service mushers, have helped protect the

Above: Built in 1929, the historic kennels building is the oldest structure at park headquarters still in use in its original purpose.

Left: A very deep bond of trust develops between the rangers and their dogs—they rely one another to get safely from place to place.

Above: *As they have for centuries, sled dogs carry their human passenger through the Alaskan wilderness.*

Right: *The sled dogs of Denali enable rangers to continue to do their jobs during the winter months in a way that does not compromise the wilderness.*

wilderness of Denali for many generations. Despite the hardships of mushing, the dogs remind us that sometimes the old way is simply the best way. They fearlessly charge through overflow ice, find a trail that's almost invisible to human eyes, and remember the way to the next patrol cabin even when the snow is flying so thickly that the human part of the team is blind. Where they once helped rangers protect the wildlife of a fledgling national park, today the sled dogs work with rangers to meet demands for winter recreation, research, and management without sacrificing the wilderness character of Denali, and in a way that preserves the park's traditions.

The history of Denali National Park is the history of human effort to set aside a wild place and preserve its wildlife, wilderness, and history so that present and future generations can touch this land and find their heritage whole. Denali's wilderness and its history are inextricably woven together, and through them both runs a team of sled dogs.

GLOSSARY OF TERMS

Alaskan Husky
Variable mix of northern-breed dogs selected for performance rather than appearance; not a standardized breed such as Siberian Husky or Malamute.

Basket Sled
Sled with an elevated basket, as opposed to a toboggan sled, which rides closer to the ground.

Brush Bow
Curved bow attached to the front of the sled; helps the sled deflect off trees and other obstacles.

"Come Gee!"/"Come Haw!"
Verbal commands given by the musher to the leader to turn the team 180 degrees, either the right (gee) or the left (haw).

Dog Yard
Home to all the dogs; where the dogs are tied out or kenneled.

Double Lead
Running two leaders side by side (as opposed to a single lead); double leads are used often to train dogs to be leaders (by putting a young, inexperienced dog with an older, experienced dog), or for dogs who feel more confident running next to a partner.

Gait
Dogs' stride and pattern of footfalls; dogs walk, lope, trot, or pace.

Gang Line

Main line running between the sled and the lead dog; line to which all the pairs of dogs are attached.

Gee Pole

Pole extending from the front right side of the sled; used by a driver on skis to help steer the sled. This method, which is not very commonly used today, helps the driver maneuver heavy loads.

Handle Bow (or Drive Bow)

Part of the sled to which the musher holds while driving; pulling the handle bow in different directions helps the musher steer.

Harness

Typically made out of a padded nylon webbing; sizing of the harness depends on the size and shape of the dog.

A. Handle bow

B. Top rail

C. Stanchions

D. Basket

E. Brush bow

F. Laminated runner

G. Doubler

H. Babiche (rawhide) lashings

I. Tooth/Claw brake (see inset)

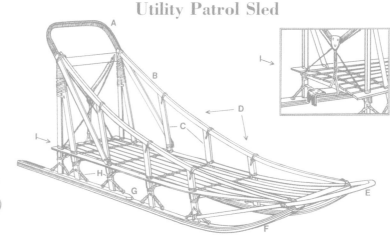

Utility Patrol Sled

"Hike!" (or "Let's Go!")
Command to go forward.

Lead
Position at the front of the team; dogs in this position follow the driver's verbal commands and guide the rest of the sled-dog team.

Neck Line
Line from the gang line to the loop on the dog's collar; helps prevent the dogs from turning around or swinging out of line.

"Straight Ahead!" (or "On By!")
Command to run past distractions such as wildlife or other dog teams.

Swing
Position immediately behind the lead dog(s); helps steer the team. Good swing dogs make wide turns at corners to prevent the sled and team from running into obstacles (such as trees).

Ski-jouring
Sport in which dogs pull a person on skis rather than a sled; ski-jourers typically use one, two, or three dogs.

Sled Bag
Canvas or nylon bag fitted to the bed of the sled; used to contain gear and hold it firmly on the sled.

Snow Hook
Steel anchor attached to the sled; stomped into the trail, it helps secure the team.

Snub Line
Line used by the musher to secure the sled to a tree or post (usually with a quick-release knot) prior to take-off or when stopped on the trail.

Stake-out Line (or Picket Line)
Long cable or chain with individual shorter cables or chains attached to it; used to secure the dogs at night while out on patrol.

Team
Position behind swing; dogs in this position provide much of the team's power. There may be several pairs of team dogs.

Toboggan Sled
A sled type, typically with a plastic bed elevated just slightly above the runners.

Tooth Brake (or Claw Brake)
Metal structure between the runners; used to help stop or slow the team down. When the musher applies downward pressure, the metal claw or teeth dig into the snow.

Track Brake
Flat square of rubber (commonly made from snow-machine track) positioned between the runners on which the musher stands; can be stepped on to slow the team down. When going down hills, the musher will usually stand on the track brake to prevent the sled from catching up with or overrunning the dogs.

Tug Line
Line running from the back of the dog's harness to the gangline; the pulling force of the tugline is distributed to the gangline.

Wheel
Position nearest the sled; dogs in this position are commonly the team's biggest, as they take the brunt of the stress in starts, stops, and maneuvering the sled's load around corners.

"Whoa!"
Command to stop, often repeated several times in conjunction with pressure from the tooth brake.

TO FIND OUT MORE. . .

The sled dogs of Denali are on the World Wide Web! Check in on the dogs at www.nps.gov/dena/

For other information about sled dogs and/or Denali National Park and Preserve, please refer to the following:

Balzar, John. *Yukon Alone*. New York: Henry Holt and Company, 1999.

Cary, Bob and Gail de Marcken. *Born to Pull*. Duluth, MN: Pfeifer-Hamilton Publishers, 1999.

Collins, Miki and Julie. *Dog Driver: A Guide for the Serious Musher*. Loveland, CO: Alpine Publications, 1991.

Hoe-Raitto, Mari and Carol Kaynor. *Skijor with Your Dog*. Fairbanks, AK: OK Publishing, 1991.

Mushing Magazine website: http://www.mushing.com

Ungermann, Kenneth A. *The Race To Nome*. Sunnyvale, CA: Press North America/Nulbay Associates, 1963.

Winter Patrol: Denali by Dogsled (video). Anchorage: Alaska Geographic Association, 1999.